First Holy Communion

PREPARING

CELEBRATING

REMEMBERING

Text by
FRANCES C. HEEREY, S.C.H.

Illustrations by
RITA GOODWILL

The Regina Press
New York

Nihil Obstat: Rev. Msgr. John A. Alesandro, J.C.D.
          Censor Librorum
          October 6, 1982

Imprimatur: Most Reverend John R. McGann, D.D.
          Bishop of Rockville Centre
          October 12, 1982

Note: The Nihil Obstat and Imprimatur are official declarations that
          this material is free of doctrinal or moral error. They do not
          imply any endorsement of the opinions and statements con-
          tained in the work.

Copyright © 1983 by The Regina Press

ISBN: 0-88271-057-5

All rights reserved. No part of this book may be reproduced in any form
without permission in writing from the publisher.

PRINTED IN BELGIUM

NAME Kimberly Sirok

I was born on Sept. 15, 1985

I was Baptized on December 15, 1985

I received my First Holy Communion on

Feb. 7, 1993

"Anyone who loves me will be true to my word, and my Father will love him; we will come to him and make our dwelling place with him."

JOHN 14:23

Table of Contents

Preface

Your word is my delight and the joy of my heart.

JEREMIAH 15:16

Dear Children and Parents,

To celebrate is to give honor to someone special. Our First Holy Communion Day is the occasion when we are honored to receive Jesus' Body and Blood. Jesus is the Son of God. Jesus is the Word of God.

Jesus loved God our Father and He loved people. It can be imagined that He often went as a child to the market place with His Mother Mary and His foster-father Joseph. Later on, as an adult, He most likely spent time among the stalls speaking with the shoppers and vendors. Jesus loved people.

This is a celebration book. It is intended to bring Jesus into the minds and hearts of children in a way that will never be forgotten.

The text and illustrations are presented for children who have been prepared to receive their First Holy Communion and for those who have already celebrated that momentous occasion. Here, in review, they can meet Jesus, the Word of God, who entered their hearts in joy and remains with them in sheer delight.

I AM SPECIAL

PREPARING

God shared life with me through my parents. Life is a wonderful gift.

He calls me by my name

---

because He loves me. I have goodness in me because He made me in His image and likeness. God calls me to use my special talents in the best way possible.

To live I need: food, clothing, shelter, love, peace. God calls me to help him care for the whole world and everything in it. He calls me to a spirit of justice and He wants me to have all I need.

CELEBRATING

O God, you are so wonderful
You know me like a friend.
Even before I speak you know what I will say.
You are everywhere with me.
Your hand shall always guide me.
You shaped me in my mother's womb.
Thank you, God, for making me wonderful, too.

PSALM 139

REMEMBERING

1. **Why am I special?**

   I am special because I am made in the image and likeness of God.

2. **Who made me?**

   God our Father made me through my parents.

3. **Why did God make me?**
   God made me because He loves me.

4. **What does God want me to do?**
   God our Father wants me to love Him. He wants me to love everybody.

5. **How do I show God that I love Him?**
   I show God that I love Him by praying to Him, obeying His laws, helping Him to care for the people and things of the earth.

6. **How do I express love for people?**
   I express love for people when I try to change things that are harmful for them. This is being a just person.

7. **What do all people need?**
   People have need for food, clothing, shelter, love, peace.

8. **Do babies, old people, and handicapped people have needs?**
   Yes, they have need for food, clothing, shelter, love, and peace.

9. **Why are all people special?**
   All people are special because they are made in the image and likeness of God.

GOD

PREPARING

God has a special name. We make a sign so that we can know His name.

In the name of the *Father*
and of the *Son*
and of the *Holy Spirit*.

Three persons in one God is called the

TRINITY

We can call God by name.
God created the whole world.
We can praise God.

Jesus is the Son of God.
The Holy Spirit is the spirit of Jesus.
The Holy Spirit gives us the power to live as
   children of God.

God is present among His people.
God shares His gifts of creation with us.
God cares for all living things.

CELEBRATING

The Lord is my shepherd
I shall not want.
He lets me rest in soft green grass.
He leads me by restful waters.
He makes my heart feel fresh.
He shows me paths to walk,
because His name is love.
Even when it's dark outside
I'm not afraid, for you are here right by my side.
You give me courage. . . .

PSALM 23

REMEMBERING

1. **What are the names of the three persons in one God?**

   The names of the three persons in one God: God the Father, God the Son, God the Holy Spirit.

2. **What name do we give the divine mystery of three persons in one God?**

   We call three persons in one God the Holy Trinity.

3. **What is the name of the Son of God?**

   Jesus is the Son of God.

4. What work does the Holy Spirit do?

The Holy Spirit gives us the power to live as children of God.

5. What prayer helps us remember the names of the Trinity?

The prayer is called "The Sign of the Cross."

6. Where is God?

God is everywhere. He is especially present among His people.

7. Who created the world?

God created the world out of nothing.

8. What prayer can we say to honor God our Father?

We can pray the "Our Father."

9. Who helps us to love God and to love each other?

The Holy Spirit helps us to love God and to love each other.

10. What work does God do?

God cares for all living things. He cares for me.

11. Why did God give us the gifts of the earth?

God gave us the gifts of the earth to make us and others happy.

BIBLE

PREPARING

Stories tell us about people and events.

The BIBLE is the book all about God. It is also called Scripture or the Word of God. Reading the BIBLE is a good way to know who God is, and some of the things He has done for His people.

The BIBLE is divided into two main parts:
Old Testament and New Testament.

The Old Testament tells us how God loved His people before Jesus was born.

The New Testament tells how God loved us so much that He gave us His Son Jesus.

CELEBRATING

Keep your Bible in a special place in your home. This Word of God can be placed in the living room or in your bedroom. The BEST way to celebrate the Bible is to read from it and to think about what God is saying to you in the scriptures.

Some holy words are taken and set to music. What holy songs or hymns do you like? Perhaps songs about Jesus or Mary are some of your favorites.

Here is a prayer to celebrate the Bible:

How I love your name O Lord.
Your disciple John wrote down some of the
scriptures.
His testimony is true, because He saw the things
He wrote about Jesus.
I praise You, Jesus. Amen. Alleluia

REMEMBERING

1. **What is the Bible?**

   The Bible is a book which tells God's word to His people.

2. **What is another name used when people speak about the Bible?**

   They use the word "scripture."

3. **Why did God give us the Bible?**

   God gave us the Bible so we can get to know Him better.

4. **How is the Bible divided?**

   The Bible is divided into two main books: the Old Testament and the New Testament.

5. **Where do we find the Gospel stories about Jesus?**

   We find the gospel stories about Jesus in the New Testament.

6. **How can we respond to God's word?**

   We can respond to God's word in prayer, song, sharing it with other people, and by acting justly.

JESUS

PREPARING

Jesus is the Son of God.

Jesus is our brother. We belong to Him.

Jesus shows us how we can be good children of our heavenly Father. He teaches us how to pray. He teaches us how to act justly. He gives us the most wonderful gift of food which is Himself in Holy Communion.

JESUS LOVES US VERY MUCH.

This is a short story of the life of Jesus.

Jesus was born in Bethlehem. His mother was Mary. His foster-father was Joseph. We celebrate Jesus' birthday on Christmas Day.

Jesus played with other children in the village of Nazareth.

Joseph taught Jesus how to make things out of wood.

When Jesus became a man, a group of 12 men followed Him. He taught them about His heavenly Father. He taught them how to love other people. He did good works and performed miracles.

Jesus shared a special meal with His disciples on the night before He died. We call it the Last Supper.

This is how Jesus died. He died because He loves us and His heavenly Father. When He died He forgave us for all our sins.

Three days after Jesus died He rose miraculously from the dead. We call this His RESURRECTION.

After His resurrection from the dead, Jesus spoke with His mother and friends. He said, Peace I leave with you. My peace I give to you.

Jesus ascended into heaven and sits at the right hand of the Father. He has arranged a place for us in His kingdom in heaven.

CELEBRATING

Oh, how I love you, Jesus!
My heart is bursting with LOVE for you.
You gave me your love,
And you showed me your life
And forever you take care of me!

Oh, how I thank you, Jesus.
My heart is bursting with THANKS to you.
You gave me my life
And you gave me my home
And forever I shall live with you.

Oh, how I praise you, Jesus.
My heart is bursting with PRAISE of you.
You gave me this world
And you gave me good friends.
And forever I shall PRAISE you,
Joyfully shouting:

I LOVE YOU, JESUS
I THANK YOU, JESUS
I PRAISE YOU, JESUS
AMEN
ALLELUIA

REMEMBERING

1. Who Is Jesus Christ?

Jesus is the Son of God, the second Person of the Blessed Trinity.

2. Where was Jesus born?

Jesus was born in Bethlehem, almost 2,000 years ago.

3. Is Jesus God?

Jesus is God and He is also man.

4. Who were the people who visited Him when He was a baby?

The shepherds and the Magi from the east.

5. Why did Jesus become Man?

Jesus became a man because He loves us and He wants to be with us. He wants to show us how to live.

6. What are some of the things Jesus did?

a) He obeyed His mother Mary and His foster-father Joseph.
b) He prayed to our heavenly Father.
c) He took care of people who were in need.
d) He gave peace to everyone.

7. **How can we be like Jesus?**

We can be like Jesus by helping people in need, caring for babies, old people, and handicapped people. We must try to share what we have with people who have nothing.

8. **How is Jesus present to us today?**

Jesus is present with His people in the Church, in the sacraments, especially in the Holy Eucharist.

9. **When did Jesus die?**

Jesus died on Good Friday.

10. **Why do we celebrate Easter?**

We celebrate Easter to honor Jesus' resurrection from the dead.

11. **Why do we celebrate Ascension Thursday?**

We celebrate Ascension Thursday to honor the day that Jesus ascended into heaven to be with His heavenly Father.

12. **Will Jesus come again?**

Yes, Jesus will come again on the last day; then He will judge the living and the dead.

GOD'S FAMILY

PREPARING

Another name for God's Family is the Church. God loves His family, the Church.

The Catholic Church is a community of people who praise and worship God, who care for one another, who celebrate the sacraments. Some people who take care of the Catholic church are: Our Holy Father the Pope, Cardinals, Bishops, Priests, Deacons, Sisters, Brothers, and other members of the laity.

To be good persons in the church we must be good to all people. We are to let the light of our good deeds shine for all to see. We became members of the Church at Baptism when our parents said "Yes." At that time the community, the church, *welcomed* us. They promised to help us know and love Jesus. This is done through certain signs called sacraments.

CELEBRATING

Let the prayer of Saint Francis of Assisi be a prayer
that I pray for the family, the church.

Lord, make me an instrument of your peace.
Where there is hatred, let me sow love;
where there is injury, pardon;
where there is doubt, faith;
where there is despair, hope;
where there is darkness, light;
where there is sadness, joy.

O Divine Master, grant that I may seek not so
    much
to be consoled as to console;
to be understood as to understand;
to be loved as to love;
for it is in giving that we receive;
it is in pardoning that we are pardoned;
and it is in dying that we are born to eternal life.
                                        Amen.

REMEMBERING

1. What is the Catholic Church?

The church is God's family. The members of the church pray together, worship God, follow His Son Jesus who started the Church, and they care for one another.

2. Who is the head of the Catholic Church?

Our Holy Father the Pope is the head of the Catholic Church.

3. When did you become a member of the Catholic Church?

I became a member of the Catholic Church on the day I was baptized.

4. What are the sacraments of the church?

There are seven sacraments:
Baptism,
Confirmation,
Eucharist,
Penance,
Anointing of the Sick,
Holy Orders,
Matrimony.

BAPTISM

PREPARING

When we think of Baptism, we think of water.

Water is necessary for life. It supports our life and the life of plants and animals. We need it to drink and to cook our food. We use it to clean ourselves, our clothing, the things we use. Plants need it in order to grow. It is cool to drink when we are hot and thirsty. We swim in it for exercise and for fun. It helps to make us strong.

At Baptism we were given a new life in God through water and the Holy Spirit. We were baptized in the name of the Father and of the Son and of the Holy Spirit. We were given power to praise God in prayer and worship. We were welcomed into God's family and we became followers of Jesus.

CELEBRATING

When Peter who was a close friend of Jesus became the first Pope, he told the people what they should do to follow Jesus. Peter said, "You must reform your lives and be baptized, each one of you, in the name of Jesus Christ, that your sins may be forgiven; then you will receive the gift of the Holy Spirit. It was to you and your children that the promise was made and all those still far off whom the Lord our God calls." ACTS 2:37–40

Lord, I am glad that Saint Peter really listened to you when you told him how to help others become members of your church. I am happy that my parents had me baptized. I want to follow You all the days of my life, as a member of your church. Amen. Alleluia.

REMEMBERING

1. **What is Baptism?**

    Baptism is the sacrament by which we become members of the Church, receive power to pray in Christian worship, and are born to a new, everlasting life by means of water and the Holy Spirit.

2. **How is Baptism given?**

    The person baptizing pours water over the head of the person being baptized and says: "I baptize you in the name of the Father and of the Son and of the Holy Spirit."

3. **What does Baptism do?**

    Baptism gives the soul the indelible mark of the Christian; takes away original sin, all personal sin, and all punishment due to sin; it gives sanctifying grace.

EUCHARIST

PREPARING

Some of our happiest times are when we share food with others at the kitchen or dining-room table. We remember stories about other people and the good times that we have had. We thank people for what they have done and for what they are.

Jesus shared food with His people. Because He loved them, He shared bread and wine with His friends. One particular evening Jesus told them that the bread and wine were special. He told them that He would make the bread and wine become His Body and Blood.

Jesus read with his friends some stories that are in the Old Testament. The stories helped them remember good things God had done for His people; that meal was called "The Last Supper."

Jesus' friends shared in the first celebration of the Eucharist that evening. They received the Body and Blood of Jesus. They received their First Holy Communion.

Eucharist means "thanksgiving." We remember to say "thanks" to God for giving us His Son Jesus in Holy Communion. At Mass we remember that the cup contains the wine, the Blood of Jesus; that the bread is the Body of Jesus; that Jesus sacrificed His life for us on the cross.

CELEBRATING

The best way to celebrate the Eucharist is to go to Mass. This is the way we celebrate Mass:

1. We sing our song of welcome.
   Penitential Rite
2. We ask forgiveness of our sins.
   Liturgy of the Word
3. We listen to God's Word as He speaks to us in the Scriptures and in the homily.
   Liturgy of the Eucharist
4. We offer gifts of bread and wine. We offer ourselves to God.

5. We remember the words of Jesus at the Last Supper:
   > Take this, all of you, and eat it:
   > This is my Body which will be given up for you.
   > Take this, all of you and drink from it:
   > This is the cup of my Blood, the blood of the new and everlasting covenant. It will be shed for you and for all so that sins may be forgiven.
   > Do this in memory of me.

6. We receive Jesus in Holy Communion.

7. We thank and praise God our Father.

8. We receive the priest's blessing. He tells us to go out in PEACE to love and serve the Lord.

We sing our songs of welcome.

We ask forgiveness of our sins.

We listen to God's Word as He
speaks to us in the scriptures

and in the homily.

We offer our gifts of bread
and wine and ourselves.

We receive Jesus in Holy Communion.

I RESPOND TO JESUS

Jesus, my heart is filled with love for you. I thank you for the gift of yourself to me in Holy Communion. I know that you love me. I know that you care for me. I know that you give me courage and make me strong to do good things. I want to care for other people when they have needs, because you want me to care for them. Bless me, Jesus. Keep me close to you every day of my life, but especially today.   Amen.

REMEMBERING

1. What is the Holy Sacrifice of the Mass?

The Holy Sacrifice of the Mass is the sacrifice of Jesus on the Cross.

2. What happens at Mass?

At Mass Jesus changes bread and wine into His own Body and Blood. He speaks His word to us through the scriptures and the homily.

3. **What are the two main parts of the Mass?**

The two mains parts of the Mass are: The Liturgy of the Word and the Liturgy of the Eucharist.

4. **What do we remember at Mass?**

We remember to praise God our Father.
We remember that Jesus died for us.
We remember that Jesus rose to a new life.
We remember that Jesus sent us His Holy Spirit to be with us always.

5. **How do we receive Holy Communion?**

We receive Holy Communion by walking reverently up to the minister of Communion (priest, deacon, or extraordinary minister). Either, put out your tongue to receive Jesus, or, place one hand on top of the other, receive the Host in your hand and put it in your mouth.

6. **What should our hearts be like when we approach Jesus?**

Our hearts should be loving hearts, for Jesus and for all other people.

7. **What special command does the priest give us at the end of Mass?**

The priest tells us to "Go in Peace."

SACRAMENT OF RECONCILIATION

PREPARING

Occasionally we find ourselves doing or thinking things that are hurtful to other people and to ourselves. sometimes we do not do the things for others or ourselves that we are responsible for. When we do, think, or omit things on purpose, we disobey God's law of love. This is called sin. By sin we hurt others and ourselves.

How can we make up to God and to others? We can do that by being sorry and telling that to God and to others. We can tell God in the Sacrament of Penance. We must remember the most important lesson learned: *God loves us very much!* He forgives us when we confess our sins to Him.

At Confession we are welcomed back and we share PEACE with God and one another.

CELEBRATING

This is the way we celebrate the Sacrament of Penance or Reconciliation, (in 5 steps).

BEFORE CONFESSION

1. We *think* of our sins, with Jesus.
2. We are *sorry* for our sins.
3. We *decide* not to sin again.

IN CONFESSION

The priest welcomes us.
We pray the Sign of the Cross.
The priest talks to us in the name of the Father.
He reads from the scriptures.

4. We *confess* what we did wrong. The priest helps us to do better. We tell God we are sorry. The priest forgives us in the name of God and His people. He gives us a penance. We thank the priest and God.

AFTER CONFESSION

5. We *do our penance*.

A SIMPLE PRAYER

O God, I remember how wonderfully I am made.
You made me because you love me.
You made other people because you love them.
Sometimes I am not kind
    or I do not care for other people in need.
I know I have hurt them and myself.
I know I have forgotten to love you and them.
I am really sorry.
I need you, Jesus,
    to help me love our Father and other people.
I need you, Father,
    to help me follow Jesus in his way of love.
I need you, Holy Spirit,
    to help me forgive and love other people
    who hurt me.

Thank you,
    for the gift of this wonderful sacrament
    which gives me the Peace of Jesus.   Amen.

REMEMBERING

1. What is the Sacrament of Penance?

Penance is the sacrament which gives us a special way to show God we are sorry for our sins. It is an action by which God shows His mercy and forgiveness.

2. What is sin?

Sin is disobeying God's law of love deliberately.

3. What is God's law of love?

God's law of love is found in the words of Jesus:

This is the first:
Hear, O Israel! The Lord our God is Lord alone! Therefore, you shall love the Lord your God with all your heart
     with all your soul
     with all your mind
     with all your strength

This is the second:
You shall love your neighbor as yourself.

MARK 12:28

4. What are the other Commandments which God has given us?

God has given us the Ten Commandments.

5. What is Confession?

Confession is telling God that we have done certain sins and that we are sorry.

6. How does the Church bring God's forgiveness in confession?

The Church brings God's forgiveness in confession through the priest.

7. What are the special steps we take in going to confession?

1. We think of our sins.
2. We are sorry for our sins.
3. We decide not to sin again.
4. We confess what we did.
5. We do our penance.

8. What do we mean by "We do our penance?"

We say the prayers or do the activity that the priest gives us immediately after our confession.

MARY

PREPARING

When Jesus was a child His Mother Mary taught him how to walk and to talk. She fed Jesus and made clothes for him. She taught him how to pray. Mary helped Jesus grow up to be a man.

Mary's life was a journey of faith to God. Mary was a very good person. She had respect for all life —plants, animals, and people. She helped take care of people when they were in need of care. She always obeyed God's Law of Love. Mary said "Yes" to God when He chose her to be the Mother of Jesus.

Because she is our mother too, Mary prays for us. It is good to ask Mary for help. She cares for us, the brothers and sisters of her Son.

A favorite prayer of people in God's family is "The Hail Mary."

CELEBRATING

There are many ways of celebrating Mary as God's Mother and ours. Some people have little shrines with a statue of Mary. Others wear medals of Mary and they pray for her protection. Others say special prayers, especially the prayer called the ROSARY.

The rosary beads have decades. Each decade has an Our Father bead and ten Hail Mary beads. There are 15 mysteries of our Lord's life that we remember when we pray the rosary. They are divided into three sections: The Joyful Mysteries, The Sorrowful Mysteries, The Glorious Mysteries.

Pray the Rosary often. It is a prayer that Mary gave to a special saint. She asked that people say the rosary in honor of her Son, Jesus.

SPECIAL FEASTS OF MARY

ANNUNCIATION

IMMACULATE CONCEPTION

THE ASSUMPTION

THE MIRACULOUS MEDAL

REMEMBERING

1. Who is Mary?

Mary is the Mother of Jesus and the Mother of God.

2. Is Mary our Mother, too?

Yes, Mary is our mother.

3. What does Mary want us to do?

Mary wants us to follow her Son Jesus and to care for His people.

4. What are 3 special feasts we celebrate in Mary's honor?

Three feasts are: Annunciation, Immaculate Conception, Assumption.

5. What is meant by the Immaculate Conception?

The Immaculate Conception means that Mary was free from original sin when she was born.

6. What happened at the Annunciation?

The Annunciation celebrates the time when the angel Gabriel announced to Mary that she was chosen to be the Mother of Jesus.

7. What is meant by the Assumption?

The Assumption means that when Mary died she was taken body and soul directly into heaven.

PRAYER

PRAYER

Don't you like talking to your friends and listening to them when they tell you stories? Prayer is something like that. Prayer is talking to God. Prayer is listening to God. Prayer is just being with God.

Sometimes we pray alone (in room, in church, anywhere).

Sometimes we pray with others (family, friends, community).

Sometimes we pray for others (sick, lonely, elderly, handicapped).

A good way to remember the kinds of prayer we pray is to think of the word ACTS.

They stand for:

ADORATION,
CONTRITION,
THANKSGIVING,
SUPPLICATION.

A Adoration—   I adore you God, Father, Son, Holy Spirit.

C Contrition—   I confess my sins with real *sorrow*.

T Thanksgiving— I thank you, God, for all your wonderful gifts.

S Supplication— I ask you for special help for myself and others.

SPECIAL PRAYERS THAT WE SHOULD KNOW

THE OUR FATHER

Our Father who art in heaven, hallowed be thy name. Thy kingdom come. Thy will be done on earth as it is in heaven. Give us this day our daily bread and forgive us our trespasses as we forgive those who trespass against us and lead us not into temptation, but deliver us from evil.   Amen.

THE HAIL MARY

Hail Mary full of grace the Lord is with Thee. Blessed art thou among women and blessed is the fruit of thy womb Jesus. Holy Mary Mother of God pray for us sinners now and at the hour of our death.   Amen.

GLORY BE TO THE FATHER

Glory be to the Father and to the Son and to the Holy Spirit, as it was in the beginning is now and ever shall be world without end.   Amen.

AN ACT OF CONTRITION

O my God I am heartily sorry for having offended Thee and I detest all my sins because of Thy just punishment, but most of all because they offend Thee, my God, Who are all good, and deserving of all my love. I firmly resolve with the help of Thy grace, to sin no more, and to avoid the near occasions of sin.   Amen.

THE APOSTLES CREED

I believe in God, the Father Almighty, Creator of heaven and earth; and in Jesus Christ, His only Son, Our Lord; who was conceived by the Holy Spirit, born of the Virgin Mary, suffered under Pontius Pilate, was crucified, died and was buried.

He descended into hell; the third day He arose again from the dead. He ascended into heaven, sits at the right hand of God, the Father Almighty; thence He shall come to judge the living and the dead. I believe in the Holy Spirit, the Holy Catholic Church, the communion of saints, the forgiveness of sins, the resurrection of the body and life everlasting. Amen.

BLESSING BEFORE MEALS

Bless us, Lord, and these Thy gifts which we are about to receive from Thy bountiful hands, through Christ our Lord. Amen.

GRACE AFTER MEALS

We give Thee thanks Almighty God, for these Thy gifts through Christ our Lord. Amen.

JUSTICE AND PEACE

We should always remember to...

Help the elderly.   Take care of babies.

Forgive people who hurt you.
Comfort those who cry.

Provide shelter and food for other people.

Express love by trying to change things that are harmful to other people.

Assist God our Father to help all people who are in need.

COMMANDMENTS OF GOD

THE TEN COMMANDMENTS OF GOD

1 . I, the Lord, am your God. You shall not have strange gods besides me.

2. You shall not take the name of the Lord God in vain.

3. Remember to keep holy the Sabbath.

4. Honor your father and mother.

5. You shall not kill.

6. You shall not commit adultery.

7. You shall not steal.

8. You shall not bear false witness against your neighbor.

9. You shall not covet your neighbor's wife.

10. You shall not covet your neighbor's goods.

COMMANDMENTS OF THE CHURCH

1. To keep holy the day of the Lord's resurrection.

2. To receive Holy Communion frequently and the Sacrament of Reconciliation regularly.

3. To study Catholic teaching.

4. To observe the marriage laws of the Church.

5. To strengthen and support the Church.

6. To do penance.

7. To join in the missionary spirit of the Church.

SEASONS OF THE CHURCH YEAR

The family of God likes to celebrate God all year round during the seasons of the Church year. The seasons are:

Advent — Christmas
Lent — Easter
Pentecost
Ordinary Time

ADVENT

This is the time in which the community prepares for the celebration of Jesus' birthday. Advent is a happy time when we awaken our hearts by praying special prayers or by having an advent wreath or by burning a Mary candle.

Advent celebration is about four weeks long.

CHRISTMAS

Christmas is the time when we celebrate the birthday of Jesus. It is a time of gift-giving to others. Giving gifts reminds us of the best gift of all which our Father in heaven gave to us: Jesus our brother.

During the Christmas season we remember Mary the Mother of God, the Holy Family, the Epiphany when the Magi visited Jesus. We celebrate Jesus as the Prince of Peace.

LENT

Lent is the time in which the community prepares for the celebration of the death and resurrection of Jesus. It is a serious time when we look at Jesus' great care and love for us. We do penance for our sins and tell Jesus and each other "I am sorry, please forgive me."

Jesus forgives us through His suffering and death on the cross.

During Lent we get ready for the new life and joy of Easter.

EASTER

Easter is the most wonderful time when we celebrate the Resurrection of Jesus. God raised Jesus from the dead. It is a time of great joy. It is the alleluia time!

Jesus brings new life to the world. Every Sunday we celebrate the feast of the Lord's Resurrection.

PENTECOST

Forty days after Jesus was raised from the dead, He ascended into heaven where He is seated at the right hand of the Father.

Afterwards, His Mother Mary and the Disciples waited in prayer for the coming of the Holy Spirit. On the day of Pentecost they had all gathered together in one place. The Holy Spirit appeared before the Apostles in tongues of fire. He sent them out to preach to the whole world the good news of Jesus. He told them to proclaim that all who believe and are baptized shall be saved.

ORDINARY TIME

This is the rest of the time during the year when we worship God, by celebrating the Resurrection of Jesus and by listening to stories about the life and teachings of Jesus.

Jesus said,

"I WILL BE WITH YOU ALL DAYS,
EVEN UNTIL THE END OF TIME."

PRINTED IN BELGIUM BY

proost

INTERNATIONAL BOOK PRODUCTION